My First Book
of Bible Verses

My First Book of Bible Verses
Old Testament

Illustrations by Letizia Galli

*Adapted by Toby Forward from an original French
text by Francois Brossier and Danielle Monneron*

Silver Burdett Press
Englewood Cliffs, New Jersey

First published in the United States by
Silver Burdett Press, 1988

Original French text © 1987 François Brossier
and Danielle Monneron
English translation text © 1988 Simon & Schuster Limited
Illustrations © 1987 Letizia Galli

Simon & Schuster Limited, West Garden Place,
Kendal Street, London W2 2AQ

Simon & Schuster Australia Pty Limited
Sydney, New South Wales

Distributed in Canada by:
General Publishing Ltd. (trade)
30, Lesmill Road, Don Mills, Ontario M3B 2T6

Novalls (religions)
P.O. Box 9700, Terminal Ottawa, Ontario K1G 4B4

Originally published in France in 1987 by Editions du Centurion, Paris,
under the title *Ma Première Bible en Images.*

Library of Congress Cataloging-in-Publication Data

Forward, Toby, 1950—
    My first book of Bible verses.

    Adaptation of: Ma première Bible en images.
    Includes index.
    1. Bible stories, English—O.T.   I. Galli, Letizia.
II. Brossier, François. Ma première Bible en images.
III. Bible O.T. English. Selections. 1988
IV. Title.
BS551.2.F65 1988.   221.9'505   88-18450
ISBN 0-382-09743-2

Introduction

The Bible is a difficult and complex book, especially for children. It is important, however, for even the youngest child to have access to the scriptures that have been handed down from generation to generation.

In *My First Book of Bible Verses*, the important stories and themes of the Old Testament are told in simple text with radiant illustrations, and will be easily understood by very young children. The illustrations do not pretend to reflect exactly the history and architecture of biblical times. More importantly, they emphasize the meaning of the text and convey the rich symbolism of the message.

The early scriptures used a narrative style to mirror the works of God, from the creation of the world to the coming of Christ. *My First Book of Bible Verses* follows their example. Even so, the texts which are retained cannot reflect the whole of the Old Testament; in particular the Books of Proverbs, Psalms, and Prophets are missing. The texts are also not always in chronological order. *My First Book of Bible Verses* is designed for parents and children to read together. In order for parents to help a child to understand the images and themes, stories from the Old Testament are retold for children at the back of the book, together with an index of the simple words used.

empty

In the beginning,

God made heaven and earth.

The earth was shapeless and **empty**.

Genesis 1:1

breath

The **breath** of God

soared over the waters.

Genesis 1:2

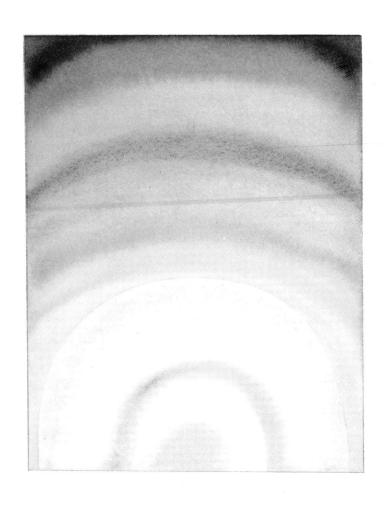

light

God separated the **light** and the darkness.

Genesis 1:4

sky

And God said,

"Let there be a roof

in the middle of the waters

to separate the waters."

God called the roof the **sky**.

Genesis 1:6,8

earth

God said,

"Let all the waters collect together

into one place,

so that the solid **earth** can appear."

Genesis 1:9

15

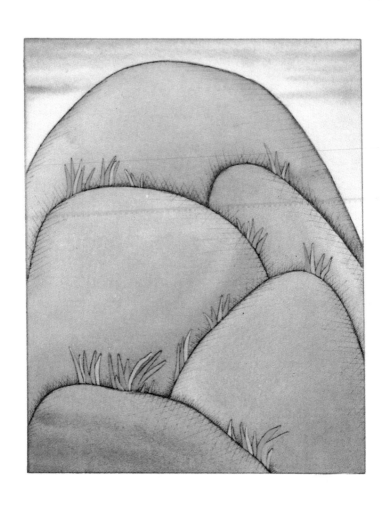

plants

God said,

"Let the earth have **plants** growing in it."

seeds

The plants grew and made **seeds**

each for its own kind.

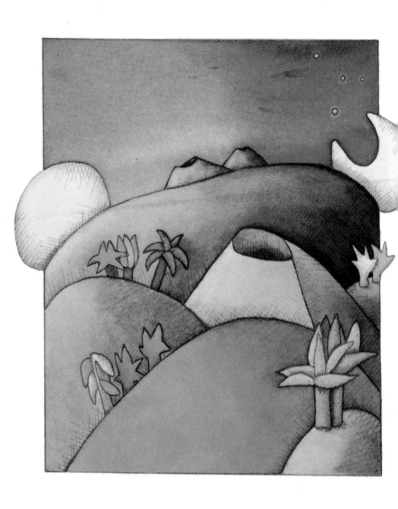

lights

God said,

"Let there be **lights** in the sky,

a big light to rule over the day

and a smaller light to rule over the night."

And he made the stars as well.

Genesis 1:14,16

sea monsters

God made all sorts of

different **sea monsters**,

everything that lives and moves

and crowds around in the water.

Genesis 1:21

birds

God made all kinds of

different **birds** that fly in the air.

beasts

God said,

"Let there be lots of animals,

great **beasts** and little **beasts**

and savage **beasts**."

Genesis 1:24

man and woman

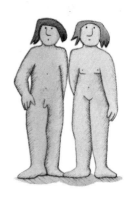

God said,

"Let's make a someone just like me."

And he made **man and woman**.

Genesis 1:26–27

creation

And God blessed the seventh day.

That day he rested,

and so did all **creation**,

everything that he had made.

garden

God planted a **garden** in Eden

and put the man and woman there.

Genesis 2:8,22

delicious fruits

God made all sorts of trees

push their way up out of the ground.

The trees were lovely to look at

and they grew **delicious fruits**.

Genesis 2:9

the tree of knowledge

And God said,

"You can eat any fruit you like

from any of the trees in the garden,

but you mustn't eat the fruit of

the tree of knowledge of good and evil."

Genesis 2:16–17

serpent

The **serpent** said to the woman,

"The day you eat the fruit of

the tree of knowledge

of good and evil, your eyes will open

and you will become like gods,

knowing good and evil."

Genesis 3:5

39

fruit of the tree

She took the **fruit of the tree**

and ate it.

And she gave it to her husband

and he ate it.

Genesis 3:6

thorns

God said to the man,

"The earth is cursed because of you!

It will give you thistles and **thorns**.

You will have to sweat

to earn your bread."

Genesis 3:17–19

ark

God said to Noah,

"You and your family

and pairs of every kind of animal

must get into the **ark**

because you are the only

good people I can find.

I am going to make the rain

fall on the earth for a long time."

Genesis 7:1-4

flood waters

Seven days later

the earth was covered with

the **flood waters.** Rain

fell upon the earth

for forty days and nights.

Genesis 7:10

dove

Noah set a **dove** free

to find out if the waters

had drained away from the earth.

olive branch

The dove came back

with an **olive branch** in her beak,

a new growth, picked fresh.

Genesis 8:11

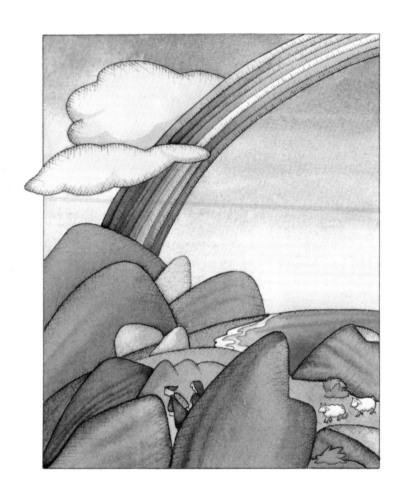

rainbow

God said to Noah,

"I'm giving you a **rainbow**

in the middle of the clouds

as a sign of my promise

that I will never again

send another flood to destroy the earth."

Genesis 9:13

tower

People said to one another,

"Come on, let's build a city

with a great **tower**

whose top will touch the sky.

We'll make a name for ourselves."

Genesis 11:4

language

God said,

"I will mix up and muddle the **language**."

The humans gave up building their town.

That's why it's called Babel,

because it was there that God

mixed up the languages of the people

who live on the earth.

Genesis 11:7-9

journey

God said to Abraham,

"Leave your own country.

Leave your family

and the place that your father lived

and go to the place that I show you.

I will make your name great.

All the families in the world

will bless themselves through you."

So Abraham set off

on his **journey**.

Genesis 12:1–4

stars

God said to Abraham,

"Look at the sky and count the **stars**,

if you can . . .

You will have more descendants

than there are stars!"

Abraham believed in God and trusted him.

Genesis 15:5–6

tent

God appeared to Abraham

by the oaks of Mamre

while he was sitting outside his **tent**.

Abraham raised his eyes and saw

three men standing in front of him.

Genesis 18:1–2

cakes

Abraham went to find Sarah in the tent

and said to her,

"Bake some **cakes**."

son

God said to Abraham,

"One year from now

Sarah will have a **son**."

When he was born,

Abraham called him Isaac.

Genesis 18:10 and 21:3

mountain

God tested Abraham.

"Take your son, your only son, Isaac,

and go to the land of Moriah

and offer him as a sacrifice

on the **mountain**."

Genesis 22:1–2

69

wood

Abraham took the **wood** for the sacrifice and piled it onto his son Isaac.

Genesis 22:6

71

knife

Abraham stretched out his hand

and seized the **knife** to sacrifice his son.

But the Angel of God said to him,

"Do not lift your hand against your son."

ram

Abraham lifted his eyes

and saw a **ram** caught in the bushes.

He sacrificed it in place of his son.

Genesis 22:13

ladder

Jacob had a dream:

a **ladder** was resting on the earth

and its top touched the sky.

Genesis 28:12

well

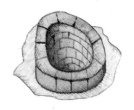

His brothers saw that Joseph

was their father Jacob's favorite son

and so they hated him.

They plotted together to kill him

and they threw him into a **well**.

caravan

His brothers pulled Joseph

from the well

and sold him to

a group of traders traveling in a **caravan**.

The traders took him to Egypt.

Genesis 37:28

slaves

The Egyptians made the Hebrews

their **slaves**

and made their lives bitter

with forced labor.

Exodus 1:13–14

the Nile River

Pharaoh gave an order to his people:

"Throw all the baby boys of the Hebrews

into **the Nile River**."

Exodus 1:22

rush basket

A Hebrew woman

put her baby son in a **rush basket**

and set it afloat

on the Nile amongst the reeds.

Exodus 2:3

Moses

Pharaoh's daughter discovered the baby.

She was sorry for him

and looked after him.

She called him **Moses** because

she had pulled him out of the water.

Exodus 2:6,10

burning bush

When he was older

Moses kept sheep for his father-in-law.

The Angel of God appeared

in the middle of a fire blazing in a bush.

Moses looked

and though the bush was on fire

it was not being destroyed by the flames.

God called from the **burning bush**

and said to him, "Go!

You must take my people out of Egypt."

Exodus 3:1–4,10

lamb

God said to Moses,

"Let every house take a **lamb**

Mark your doorposts with its blood

and eat it in great haste.

When I see the blood,

I will pass over you

and I will not destroy your firstborn sons

when I smite the land of Egypt.

It is the Passover of God."

Exodus 12:3,11

93

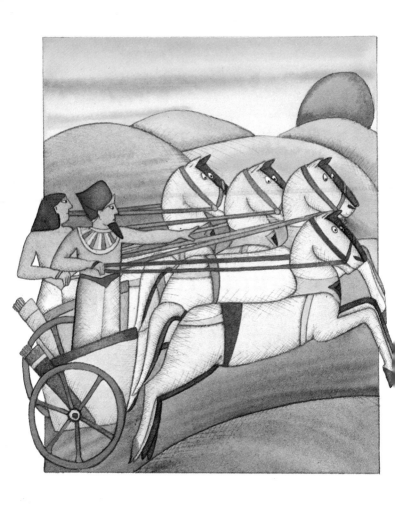

chariots

The people of Israel set off.

Pharaoh took all the **chariots** of Egypt

and set off to chase

the people of Israel.

Exodus 12:37 and 14:7–8

pillar of cloud

The Egyptians caught up with
the people of Israel while they were
encamped by the shore of the sea.
A **pillar of cloud** moved from
in front of them and placed itself
between the camp of the Israelites
and the camp of the Egyptians.

Exodus 14:9,19–20

staff

God said to Moses,

"Raise your **staff**.

Stretch out your hands over the sea.

Split it in two."

Exodus 14:16

wall of water

The waters split

and the people of Israel

went through the sea

without even wetting their feet.

There was a **wall of water**

to the left and the right of them.

Exodus 14:21–22

sea

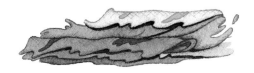

The waters rushed back

and swept over the whole

of Pharaoh's army,

his chariots, and his men

who had all gone through the **sea**

to chase the people of Israel.

Exodus 14:28

people

That day,

God saved Israel

from the hand of Egypt.

The **people** believed in God

and trusted Moses.

They sang a song to God.

Exodus 14:30–31 and 15:1

desert

The people of Israel

blamed Moses and his brother Aaron.

"You didn't have to

bring us out into the **desert**

for all the people to die of hunger."

Exodus 16:2–3

107

manna

God said to Moses,

"Look, I'm going to make bread

rain down from the sky."

The next morning the ground was covered

with something white like frost.

The people of Israel said,

"It is **manna**."

Moses told them,

"It is the bread God has given."

Exodus 16:4,13–15

water

God said to Moses,

"Hit the rock with your staff.

Water will come out

for the people to drink."

Exodus 17:6

smoke

Moses climbed toward God.

Mount Sinai was covered in **smoke**

because God

had come down in the fire.

Exodus 19:3,18

stone tablets

God said to Moses,

"I'm going to give you the **stone tablets**,

the Law and the Ten Commandments

I have written

for you to teach the people."

Exodus 24:12

golden calf

God said,

''Go back down.

The people are corrupt.

They have made a **golden calf**.

They are bowing down and worshiping it.''

Moses burned with anger.

He grabbed the calf and melted it

and ground it to powder.

Exodus 32:7-8, 19-20

land

Moses climbed from the foothills of Moab

up to Mount Nebo overlooking Jericho.

God showed him all the **land**.

"This land you see is the land I promised

to Abraham and to Isaac and to Jacob,

to you and to your people for all time.

I have let you see it,

but you will never go into it."

That was where Moses died.

Deuteronomy 34:1,4–5

Ark of the Covenant

God said to Joshua,

"I will be to you as I was to Moses."

Joshua said to the people of Israel,

"Look, the **Ark of the Covenant** of God

will go across the Jordan ahead of us."

Joshua 3:7,9,11

dry feet

When the priests who carried the Ark

got to the bank of the Jordan

the water stopped

and mounted up like a wall.

So the people of Israel walked across

with **dry feet**.

Joshua 3:15–17

123

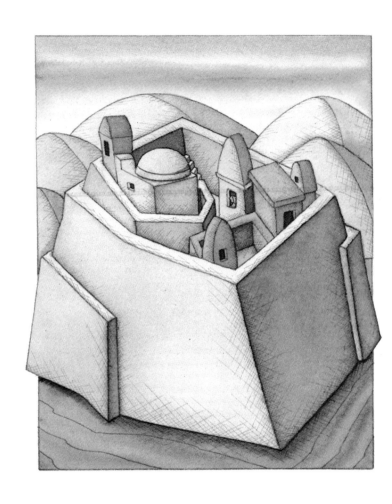

walls

The **walls** of Jericho

were locked against the people of Israel

and they could not go in or out.

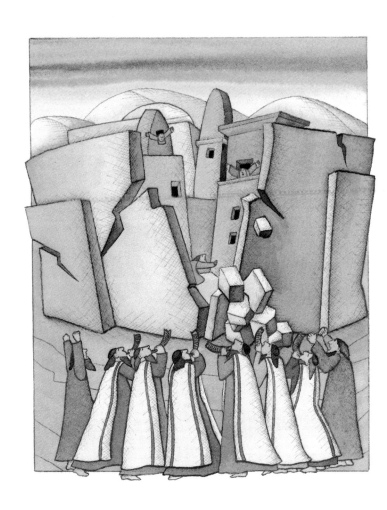

horns

The priests blew on their **horns**

and Joshua said to the people,

"God has given you the city."

The people shouted at the top of their voices

and the walls fell down.

Joshua 6:16,20

temple

Hannah took Samuel

to the **temple** at Shiloh and said,

"You, God, answered my prayer

and gave him to me.

Now, I return him to you."

1 Samuel 1:24,27–28

129

lamp

The **lamp** of God's presence

was still burning.

God called Samuel, who answered,

"Speak, your servant is listening."

1 Samuel 3:3–4,10

king

When Samuel grew older

God said to him,

"I am sending you to Bethlehem

to see Jesse because

I have chosen a **king** from among his sons."

Jesse showed Samuel seven of his sons

and Samuel said,

"God has not chosen any of these."

1 Samuel 16:1,10

oil

Jesse went to find his youngest son, David.

Then God said,

"This is him. Anoint him."

Samuel took the horn, full of **oil**,

and poured it on him.

1 Samuel 16:12–13

sword and spear

David said to Goliath,

"You are coming against me

with a **sword and spear**

but I am fighting with

the God of armies on my side."

1 Samuel 17:45

slingshot

He plunged his hand into his bag

and pulled out a stone.

He flung the stone from his **slingshot**

and it sank into the Philistine's head.

Goliath fell down

on his face on the ground

and David killed him.

1 Samuel 17:49

dance

David took the Ark of God

up to Jerusalem with shouts of joy.

He wore only a linen cloth

and in his delight

he did a magnificent **dance** for God.

2 Samuel 6:12,14

throne

God said,

"Your house and your **throne**

shall always stand before me.

I will never stop loving you."

2 Samuel 7:16

stone

King Solomon ordered

great blocks of **stone**

to be dug out and cut up

to make the foundations

of the temple of God.

1 Kings 5:31

mountain of God

The word of God

was sent to the prophet Elijah.

"Go to the **mountain of God**

and wait for God

so that you can see him pass."

1 Kings 19:11

gentle breeze

At God's approach

there was a hurricane.

God was not in the hurricane,

nor in the earthquake,

nor in the fire,

but he was in the murmuring

of a **gentle breeze**.

1 Kings 19:11–12

army

Nebuchadnezzar, King of Babylon,

attacked Jerusalem with his great **army**.

He burned down the temple,

the palace, and all the houses,

and he took away the people

into captivity.

2 Kings 25:1,9,11

shelter

"Our God has not forgotten us.

He has given us back our lives,

because he has allowed us

to rebuild the temple of God.

We shall have a safe **shelter**

in Jerusalem," Ezra said.

Ezra 9:9

the book

All the people gathered together

like a single person.

They asked Ezra the Scribe

to read to them

from **the book** of the Law of Moses.

He read from dawn until noon.

Nehemiah 8:1,3

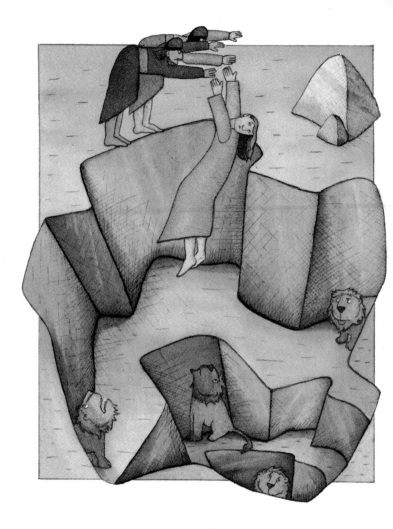

pit

The King ordered them to take Daniel

and throw him into a **pit** of lions.

He said to Daniel,

"You never stop worshiping your God.

Let him save you!"

Daniel 6:17

lions

As soon as it was morning

the King rushed to the pit

and called to Daniel.

Daniel answered,

"My God sent an angel

to close the **lions'** jaws."

Daniel 6:20–23

tempest

Jonah went to sea

to run away from God.

But God let loose

a raging storm over the sea

and raised up a **tempest**.

The sailors were terrified.

They seized Jonah

and threw him overboard.

Suddenly the fury of the storm passed.

Jonah 1:3–5,15

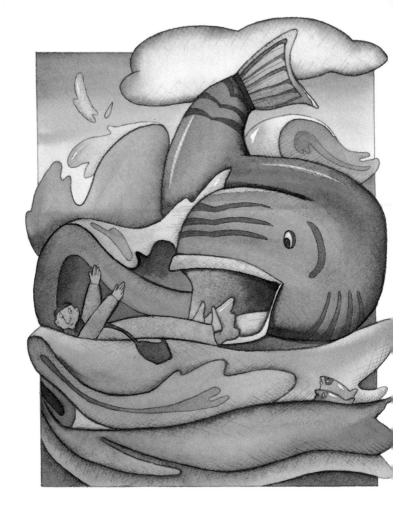

fish

God commanded a great **fish**

to swallow Jonah.

Jonah stayed

for three days and three nights

in the belly of the fish.

In the belly of the fish he prayed to God.

Jonah 2:1-2

dry land

So God spoke to the fish again

and it spewed Jonah onto **dry land**.

Jonah got up

and obeyed the Word of God.

Jonah 2:11 and 3:3

the way

In those days,

John the Baptist appeared.

John is the one

the prophet Isaiah spoke about

when he said,

"A voice cries out in the desert—

Prepare **the way** of the Lord.

Make his path smooth."

Matthew 3:1,3

The Best-Loved
Bible Stories

The Story of Creation

It was all a jumble. It was a mess and a muddle. So God
got to work. He breathed gently over the tumbling waters
and made some sense out of it all. He pushed the darkness
all to one side and made it wait there until he was ready
for it. So the light broke through, clear as clear, and it was
day at last. And God liked that, and he thought it was good.
And it was. Now that it was day there was a beautiful blue
curve stretching up over everything. God said, "That's the
sky." There was the sky up at the top and the waters down
at the bottom, and sometimes it rained from the sky to the
waters, and God liked that as well, and thought that it was
good. And it was.

Then, just as he pushed the darkness away to show the
light, he pushed some of the water away to show the land.
God liked the land. "That's good as well," he said. And it
was. "It could do with something else, though," he thought.
And immediately small plants, grasses, and herbs pushed
their way through the soil. "I like those," he said. "They're
good." And they were. So he made lots of different ones: big

ones and small ones, dark green and pale yellow, rich deep browns and heavy reds. There were ripe sweet fruits and juicy berries. "Good," he said. "It's all very good." And it was.

The light came and the dark came. And the light and the dark again. And God liked them both. So, he made the sun to tell the light when to come, and the moon and the stars to tell the dark when to come. "That's good, " he thought, And it was.

Then God looked into the water and thought it could do with something. He made great sea monsters — huge, lumbering things that could plunge deep into the water where it was dark and cold, and then lift their heads and move up and leap right out of the water again. It was good. So God made some more sorts, sharks with sharp teeth, and swordfish with long pointed noses, and some with wide, flat fins like wings so that they could fly through the waters. They loved the water. God continued making more and more things: tiny, darting fish and fat, floppy ones. They were blue and red and gold and silver. They were spotted and striped. "They're good," said God. And they were.

The air seemed a bit empty so God decided to make creatures that fly. There were doves and ravens, herons and seagulls, hummingbirds and wrens, woodpeckers and robins. There were even parrots. And their colors were even brighter than the fish. They soared and swept through the air. They flapped and flew. They perched and preened.

"This is good," said God. And it was.

Then God made other animals: elephants and mice, fierce animals and placid beasts. They barked and howled and groaned and growled and bayed and brayed and snorted and sniffed and hissed and snuffled and bleated and blew and trumpeted and grunted. It was a lot of noise. "That's good," said God.

Adam and Eve

Then God made creatures just like him. He made a man and a woman and gave them the world. All the muddle was gone. God had sorted it all out and made it the way he wanted it. And it was good. So God had a rest from all his work.

Then God planted a garden for the man and the woman and all the animals and birds and fishes to live in. No one was afraid of anyone else and they lived together in peace. The trees and bushes grew delicious fruits and God said the woman and man could eat any of them that they liked. Nothing hurt them. "This is good," they thought. And it was.

But there was one tree in the very middle of the garden. This was the tree that grew special fruit that told you what was good and what was bad. "Never eat that fruit," said God. He said it kindly, but they knew he meant it.

There was a snake in the garden. The snake was very crafty. He sidled up to the man and the woman and whispered to them in a sly hissing voice. He told them to eat the special fruit that God had said they should not eat. "It will make you like God," he said. "You'll know about good and bad." And they ate it. They both did. Just as the snake told them to do.

When God found out what they had done he was sad. He took the man and the woman out of the garden. Now there were thistles and thorns, the animals were fierce, and the man and the woman had to look after themselves. God and the garden seemed a long way away and a long time ago. Sometimes they forgot about God and the garden altogether. But God didn't forget about them. "This isn't so good," they said to themselves. And it wasn't.

Noah's Ark

God watched the world and saw things get worse. But Noah was a good man. So God said to Noah, "I shall make an arrangement with you, and I shall save you.

"Build yourself an ark." So Noah built the ark, a huge ship made of lovely, hard, scented wood. He got pairs of each type of animal that God had made and he put them two by two, male and female, into the ark. Then he got in with his family and shut all the doors, very tightly.

It began to rain. Everything was covered with water. It rained and rained and rained. Only the ark was safe. Everything else was swept away. Whenever Noah and his family peeped out of the ark all they could see was rain above and water below.

After a long time the rain stopped and the ark floated about waiting. Then, at last, Noah took a dove and let it out of the roof of the ark and it flew away. "Let's see," said Noah. When the dove came back it had a twig in its beak. "It's a bit of olive tree," said Noah. "The flood's gone." So they opened up the ark, and they were on the top of a mountain. All the land was back again and all the mess had gone.

Then Noah built an altar to thank God for saving him. God was pleased. "That won't happen again, I promise," he said. "Look. Just to remind you of my promise to you." And God drew a beautiful bow in the sky: red and orange and yellow and green and blue and indigo and violet. "That's lovely," said Noah. And it was lovely.

The Tower of Babel

All the people spoke the same language. In one town the people started to build a tower. "Right up to the sky and into heaven," they said. "We want to be like gods ourselves." God didn't like this. The tower was getting very tall. So God said, very quietly, "Make a jumble of all the language." Suddenly, everyone said something different when they spoke. They couldn't understand each other at all. All they heard was babble. They called the place Babel because that was where the babble began.

Abraham

Abraham was very old when God started to talk to him. "Go where I tell you," said God. "Where?" said Abraham. "Where I tell you," repeated God. So Abraham went and God said that years later people would be blessed because of Abraham. Abraham trusted God and left his home with his wife Sarah. God promised to look after him.

One night Abraham was thinking about how he had no children to follow him when he died. He was sad. God said to Abraham, "Look at the stars. Can you count them? There are thousands of them." Abraham agreed that there were a lot. "You will have more children and grandchildren and great-grandchildren and so on than there are stars in the sky." "Good," said Abraham and he trusted God even though he and Sarah were very old.

Abraham and his family put up their tents by the oaks at Mamre. One day, Abraham sat in the entrance to his tent, enjoying the shade and God came to him. Abraham looked up, and there were three men standing in front of the tent. Abraham ran out of the tent to meet them and bowed down before God. Then Abraham told Sarah to make some cakes and they all ate together.

God said to him, "In one year I shall return and Sarah will have a son." Sarah laughed because it seemed so silly at their age. But God was right and one year later Sarah had a baby and she called him Isaac. Isaac means "laughter."

Abraham and Isaac

God tested Abraham. "Take Isaac, go to Moriah, and offer him to me on the mountain there as a burned sacrifice." Abraham was very sad. When he got to the mountain he cut the wood to make a fire and he put Isaac on it. He tied him up and stretched out his hand, holding a knife.

"Abraham," called God. "Don't touch your son Isaac with that knife. I know that you fear God." Abraham was very glad and saw a ram caught in the bushes. So Abraham sacrified the ram instead of Isaac. And Abraham knew that God loved him and he trusted God.

Jacob's Ladder

Sometimes people thought that God was a long way off and that he didn't want anything to do with them anymore. One day, Jacob, the son of Isaac, went on a journey. As the sun set he stopped to sleep. As he slept he dreamed that he saw a ladder, and the bottom touched the earth where he was lying and the top touched heaven. Jacob was in awe. "God is present," he thought. "We're still in touch."

Joseph

Everyone could see that Joseph was Jacob's favorite son. So, of course, his brothers hated him. They decided to kill him, so they threw him into a deep pit. Just then a caravan came along—camels with heavy burdens on their backs, and traders and slaves, on their way to Egypt. The brothers were frightened to kill Joseph, so they sold him to the traders instead. So Joseph was taken to Egypt and he met Pharaoh—the King.

Although Joseph was a slave, Pharaoh loved him and he became rich. All of Joseph's family joined him in Egypt and they all had children, and soon there were many of them. They were called Hebrews and were made to work very hard and treated badly. One day Pharaoh became frightened that the Hebrews would stop being slaves and would take over because there were so many of them. So, he said that all the baby boys of the Hebrews had to be thrown into the Nile, the great river that runs through Egypt, and they would be drowned.

One Hebrew woman hid her baby boy. She made a basket and put him in it and hid it in the rushes at the riverside. Pharaoh's daughter found the baby and loved him right away. She called him Moses, because she said she had saved him from the water.

Moses

One day Moses saw an Egyptian beating a Hebrew. He was so upset that, when no one was looking, Moses killed the

Egyptian and hid his body in the sand. Then Moses was afraid. Pharaoh would be angry. So Moses ran away and became a shepherd.

One night, while he was watching his sheep he saw a bush blaze up on fire. But the bush didn't burn up, it just blazed and blazed. God spoke to Moses from the middle of the fire. "I am the God of Abraham and Isaac and Jacob," said God. "It's time to take the Hebrews out of Egypt." God told Moses how to get the people ready. "Every house is to cook a lamb. Eat it standing up, with your cloak on and your staff in your hand. It's time to go now. This is the Passover night."

When they left, Pharaoh gathered his army and chased them in chariots to bring them back to be slaves again. "Where are we going?" asked Moses. "Follow the pillar of cloud," God told him. So they followed it until they got to the seashore. Then it moved around behind them and hid them from Pharaoh and the Egyptians. Then they were stuck, with the sea in front and the army behind. Moses began to worry. "Stretch out your arm and raise your staff," said God. All night, the wind blew and the water cleared away. The Hebrews walked across without even getting their feet wet. When Pharaoh and his army chased them onto the seabed the waters began to rush back and the Egyptians were all drowned. Seeing this, the Hebrews knew that God would help them when they got into trouble and they sang songs to him to thank him.

Manna from Heaven

There was a long way to go before they would get to the place that God had prepared for them. They had to travel through hot desert, without enough to eat or drink. Sometimes they wished they were back in Egypt and they complained to Moses and doubted God. "Don't worry," he said. "God will save us." And he prayed to God.

"All right," agreed God. "I will give you a sign. In the morning go and look on the ground." When they woke up there was a thin layer of food everywhere for them to gather up. There was enough for everyone, but there was none left over. "It's called manna," said God. Moses knew it was the bread of God. "Now," said God, "Bang your staff against that rock." The water poured out and everyone could drink again. Then everyone knew that God was with them.

Then Moses went up the mountain to talk to God directly. The mountain roared and shook. Smoke billowed out. Moses was impressed. God gave Moses some laws written on stone so that they could keep them safe. "These laws are a sign of our agreement," said God. "You're going to need them."

"Now?" asked Moses. "Already?" "That's right," said God. "They've forgotten me already. Just while we've been talking."

When he got down from the mountain Moses saw what God meant. The Hebrews had made a calf out of gold and were bowing down and worshiping it. Moses was very angry. He made them burn the calf to ashes and then grind the ashes into powder. He sprinkled the powder into water and made them drink it. Then, he taught them the laws that God had given them.

God was pleased with the way that Moses had helped him so he showed him a view from another mountain. There was a wide river, called the Jordan, and then a beautiful country on the other side. "That's it," he said. "That's what I promised to Abraham and Isaac and Jacob." "I'm glad I've seen it," said Moses, because he knew he was too old to go any further, too old to go into the beautiful land. He died there, looking at where God had led him.

Joshua

After the death of Moses, God said to Joshua, "You are my servant now." The Hebrews had a very special box inside which they kept the pieces of stone with the laws that God had given to Moses on the mountain. They called it the Ark of the Covenant because it reminded them that they had an agreement with God.

"Take all the people into the country I've brought you to," said God. "How can we get across the river?" asked Joshua. "Don't worry," said God. "Take the Ark of the Covenant to the edge of the river." So the priests picked up the Ark of the Covenant and led all the people to the river bank. Then, the waters rolled up like a carpet and the people all walked across without even getting their feet wet. It was just like when Pharaoh chased them from Egypt.

The Walls of Jericho

In this new land no one made them very welcome. The cities had big walls around them and the people inside locked the gates against the Hebrews so they couldn't get in.

"Get the priests to march around the walls, blowing trumpets and horns," said God. So they all stood around the outside of the city walls and the priests blew as hard as they could on their ram's horns. The noise was terrible. "Get the others to shout," said God. So they all shouted while the priests kept blowing. And the walls just crumbled and tumbled and fell down and the city was open to everyone. The Hebrews had arrived.

Samuel

Hannah took her son Samuel to the temple at Shiloh. "I'm leaving you here" she explained to him. "I asked God to give me a son," she said, "and he gave you to me. Now, God, I give him back to you."

Samuel lived in the temple with Eli the priest. He even slept there. All night there was a lamp burning. One night he woke up because he heard a voice. "Samuel, Samuel," it said. He soon understood because Eli had told him what to say. "Yes, God?" he answered. "I hear you and am your servant." "That's good," thought God.

When Samuel grew older God had a job for him. "Go to Bethlehem," he said. "Find a man called Jesse. One of his sons is going to be the king."

Jesse was pleased when Samuel arrived, and he brought his sons so that Samuel could look at them. There were seven altogether. They were all great big men. Samuel thought that any one of them could be a king. "Which one?" he asked God. "None of them. Let me see some more," replied God. "Are there any more?" Samuel asked Jesse. "Only David," said Jesse. "You don't want him." "Let me see him," said Samuel. David was still only a young boy but was very handsome. "That's the one," said God. So Samuel poured oil from a horn onto David to show that God had chosen him and that one day he would be king.

David and Goliath

The Philistines were at war with the Hebrews. Their best soldier, a giant called Goliath, was very frightening. He jeered at the Hebrews. So David went out and shouted at him. "You're big and strong, and you've got a sword and a spear and a coat of armor." "That's right," thought Goliath. "But I've got the God of armies on my side," shouted David. Goliath smiled. Then he came forward to kill David.

David grabbed a small, smooth stone from his bag and put it into his sling and let it fly at Goliath. It hit him right in the center of his forehead and he fell to the ground. Then David killed Goliath with Goliath's own sword, and cut off his head.

Then the Hebrews fought the Philistines and won. David led them up to Jerusalem with the Ark of the Covenant. He danced and danced to show God how happy he was.

God liked the dancing a lot, but he sounded very serious when he spoke to David. "You are the king now," he said. "And your children will always be my kings."

Solomon

The next king was Solomon. He got the people to drag huge blocks of stone to the top of the hill in Jerusalem and lay solid foundations and build a temple for them to worship God in. He was very proud of it.

Elijah

Many years later people thought God didn't talk to them anymore. They thought he had gone away. They had lost the pieces of stone with the laws on them, and they didn't seem to care what they did. They hurt people who stole from them; and they didn't bother to look after people who were weak and needed help. In the end they forgot about God altogether and worshiped other gods instead. Elijah was worried about this. "It's all a mess," he said to God. "How do they know where you are?" "I'll give you the answer on the mountain," said God. So Elijah went to the mountain.

There was a huge wind, bending all the trees and whipping up the dust. "Is that you?" asked Elijah. But there was no answer. Then the ground shook and Elijah couldn't stand up anymore. It was like being on a boat in a rough sea.

"That's you, isn't it?" asked Elijah. No answer. Then a fire started and Elijah was frightened. "Are you there?" But there was still no answer.

When everything had calmed down Elijah heard a small voice like a light breeze. "You are my servant," it said. "Do as I say and I will keep my promise." "I'm glad I found you," said Elijah.

Elijah did his best, but it was difficult. People thought they didn't need God. They thought it would be all right as long as they had a big army and a strong king.

One day a king with a bigger army arrived. He was called Nebuchadnezzar, the king of Babylon. He burned down the temple in Jerusalem, pulled down the houses, and took the people off to be slaves, just as they had been hundreds of years ago in Egypt.

Ezra

God waited. He wondered what the people would think. Sometimes they cried when they remembered what it had been like to be in Jerusalem and to love God. "How did we get to be so unhappy?" they asked themselves. Sometimes they dreamed that one day they would be free again and could go back to Jerusalem and build it all up again. "So you're sorry now, are you?" said God. But even though they longed for God's help, when God spoke to them they couldn't hear him clearly anymore because it was so long since they had listened to him.

"We want to hear God," they said to Ezra. So Ezra read out to them all the stories about how God made the world, and about Abraham and Isaac and Jacob and Joseph and Moses and Joshua, and about the laws on the pieces of stone, the story of God's promise. "It's his voice," they said. "That's God talking to us." "That's right," God whispered to Ezra. "That's right," said Ezra to the people. "God never abandons his people."

Daniel in the Lion's Den

Daniel was very clever and King Nebuchadnezzar loved him even though he was a Hebrew slave. He made him an important minister in his kingdom.

Daniel was faithful to Nebuchadnezzar and his son, King Darius, but many of the other ministers were jealous of him. They made the king agree to a law that said that only the king could be worshiped for thirty days. Daniel continued to worship God and this made the king very angry. Although he loved Daniel, he told him not to talk to God again or he would be put to death. So they took Daniel away and threw him into a pit full of lions.

All night the king lay awake. He was very sad about Daniel and wished he had not ordered him killed. In the morning he ran to look into the pit to see what was left of Daniel.

"I'm here," said Daniel. The king was astonished. The lions had not touched Daniel and he was safe and well. Darius told everyone that Daniel had been saved by his God.

Jonah and the Whale

Nineveh was a bad place. The people were very bad. "Go and tell them I'm very angry with them", said God to Jonah. But Jonah was frightened of what might happen to him if he went. So he ran away from God and instead of getting on the boat for Nineveh he got on a boat that was going as far away from Nineveh as possible. He didn't want the people of Nineveh to kill him. "Someone else will tell them," he thought.

There was a terrible storm. The boat was thrown about on the sea and everyone thought they would drown. They blamed Jonah because he was running away from God. "It's all my fault," said Jonah. So they threw him overboard and the storm suddenly stopped and they were safe.

A huge fish came and swallowed Jonah and he lived inside it for three days and three nights. He was very frightened, and after three days he prayed to God. "Help me, save me; forgive me even if I do not deserve it, for you love me." And God heard the prayer and the fish was sick and Jonah dropped out of its mouth onto a beach. "Now," said God, "go to Nineveh." Jonah went and told the people of Nineveh and they thanked him and asked God to forgive them, and God forgave them.

John the Baptist

The world was still a wilderness although the people of Israel remembered God's promise to them. "God is sending someone who will show you that God has kept that promise," said John the Baptist. He was a prophet who baptized people in the Jordan River. "They don't really believe me," said John "but I'll still tell them to get ready."

Index of Biblical Citations

Index

How to Read
This Book to Children

When our friends or relatives ask us "How have you been?" we usually respond with a narrative: "Well, last month I did this—and just this week, this happened to me," and so on.

We tell true stories like that in order to communicate who we are, what we have done, and who is important to us. The Bible is a collection of stories about God's people in the past—who they were, what they did, and how God was important to them.

You and your child are a part of God's people in the present day. Just as the stories of your personal past reveal who you are and how you grew that way, so the stories of the Bible are a part of us. They throw light on God's plan of love for our human lives; they describe how our ancestors, who also honored God's name, lived out that plan in their lives.

The Bible is our family album, and *My First Book of Bible Verses* is a collection of snapshots designed to introduce your child to some relatives in the faith and their adventures with God.

Use this book with your child as you would any storybook. The stories included here are among the more familiar ones from the Bible and require no special knowledge on your part. Feel free to add details to the narratives supplied in the back of this book.

You may find that a particular illustration or story will spark a question from your child that leads into a discussion. Do not be afraid to admit your ignorance on a particular point. Human beings have not changed all that much in the thousands of years covered by biblical history. We still react to God the way our ancestors in the faith did—with a combination of wonder, gratitude, fear, joy, and anxiety. Always remember the basic point that the whole Bible teaches: God loves us.

Combine your use of this book with prayer so that your child may come to appreciate that God continues to speak to us through the inspired words of the Bible. With children, prayer need not be lengthy or eloquent. Let the images and the stories inspire simple sentiments like "Thank you, God, for creating us in your image" or "Help us believe the way Abraham did."

Let your children open the book themselves to choose one of their favorite words, a picture that they prefer, or one of their favorite stories and let them retell it in their own words. After several readings, you will discover, along with your child, dozens of ways to read and enjoy *My First Book of Bible Verses.*

However you use this book, its greatest lesson will be the faith you are sharing with your child.

Imprimé en France par Aubin Imprimeur à Poitiers
Reliure SIRC à Marigny-le-Châtel (France)